Bibliographic information published by the German National Library:

The German National Library lists this publication in the National Bibliography; detailed bibliographic data are available on the Internet at http://dnb.dnb.de .

Imprint:

Copyright © 2015 GRIN Verlag
Print and binding: Books on Demand GmbH, Norderstedt Germany
ISBN: 9783668671898

This book at GRIN:

https://www.grin.com/document/418143

Shristi Tandukar

Business Research Methodology (BRM)

GRIN Verlag

GRIN - Your knowledge has value

Since its foundation in 1998, GRIN has specialized in publishing academic texts by students, college teachers and other academics as e-book and printed book. The website www.grin.com is an ideal platform for presenting term papers, final papers, scientific essays, dissertations and specialist books.

Visit us on the internet:

http://www.grin.com/

http://www.facebook.com/grincom

http://www.twitter.com/grin_com

A Research on Brand Preference of Laptop

Among Students

Shristi Tandukar

(prepared for fulfillment of MBA course)

Table of Contents

List of Tables

List of Figures

Chapter 1: Introduction

1.1 INTRODUCTION

Laptop has become a very useful device for everyone from students to profesionals.It has become a vital instrument used for studies, office works, refreshments and many more. Our daily lives have been more influenced by the laptop.

It has completely replaced the desktop computer due to its overcoming advantages over desktop computer that is its portability, battery backup in the absence of electricity, media presentations high capacity of memory, speed, less space occupancy and functionalities over desktop computer. So, nowadays laptops are more preferable than desktop.

Due the customers demand for laptop, with the innovation and change in technology, various brands of laptops with different new features are available in the market. All laptop brands have their own features and uniqueness. In today's market we find various brands of laptops available such as: Dell, Lenovo, Apple, HP, Compaq, Sony, Acer, Toshiba etc. Each available with different functions. The various brands of laptops even if differ in functions they look similar in appearance and differ in design and colour.

The students or office workers use laptops for doing their sole work. The portability of laptops allows people to do their assignments in their leisure time anytime anywhere. It helps to do many things that they cannot do with a desktop. Students and educators have found that laptops answer a lot of their needs. Previously, Laptops were only used by professionals; nowadays its popularity has increases among the students as well. And for students it has been a definite need than a luxury.

This research is conducted to know the preference of most of the MBA students use their laptop and what are the factors that influence their purchase decision, their desire and choice of particular brand of laptop.

1.2 PROBLEM STATEMENT

This research is conducted to know about the brand preference of laptops among the students. It also studies about the brand of laptop the students use, their satisfaction to their laptop the need of the students, their expectation and awareness of laptops in the MBA students.

The advancement in the technology has replaced the desktop computers by laptop. The study focusses whether Portability, battery backup in the absence of electricity, media presentations high capacity of memory, speed less space occupancy and functionalities in the laptop are the only reason to use the laptop. Various brand of laptop are launching in the market as well as the existing brand are also adding up the features in laptop to increase the reliability of their product and their sale volume. Moreover, the changing need and preferences of customer and increased competition in the market also increases the challenge for the company to meet the customers' expectation. Innovation in the features of branded laptop is a must to sustain the competition in the global market.

This kind of research helps to identify the demand of the customers particularly the students, as they are also occupying the larger share of laptops consumer market these days. It also helps to identify the potential consumers, their response towards a particular brand, factors influencing the purchase of a laptop and the performance of different brand of laptops.

1.3 RESEARCH OBJECTIVES

The major objectives of conducting this research are as follows:

- To know the brand preference of laptop among the students.
- To know the purposes of using laptop by students.
- To understand whether their requirements and expectations have been fulfilled.
- To know the factors influencing their purchase of a laptop.
- To know the student's satisfaction level from the brand of laptop they are using.
- To know why the students prefer a particular brand of laptop.
- To generate valid and consistent customer feedback.
- To know how theories match with the actual situation.
- To improve the report writing skills.

1.4 THEORETICAL FRAMEWORK

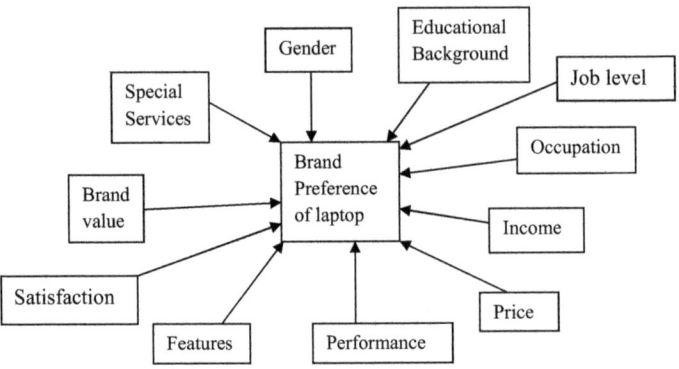

Figure1. Brand Preference model of laptops.

1.4.1. RESEARCH QUESTIONS

1. Is there any significant relationship between Gender and brand preference of laptop?
2. Is there any significant relationship between Family occupation and brand preference of laptop?
3. Is there any significant relationship between Income level and brand preference of laptop?
4. Is there any significant relationship between Price range and brand preference of laptop?
5. Is there any significant relationship between Performance and brand preference of laptop?
6. Is there any significant relationship between Brand value and brand preference of laptop?
7. Is there any significant relationship between Features and brand preference of laptop?
8. Is there any significant relationship between after sales services and brand preference of laptop?

1.4.2 RESEARCH HYPOTHESIS

1. **Null Hypothesis (H0):** There is no significant relationship between gender and brand preference of laptop.

   Alternate Hypothesis (H1): There is significant relationship between gender and brand preference of laptop.

2. **Null Hypothesis (H0):** There is no significant relationship between family occupation and brand preference of laptop.

   Alternate Hypothesis (H1): There is significant relationship between family occupation and brand preference of laptop.

3. **Null Hypothesis (H0):** There is no significant relationship between income level and brand preference of laptop.

   Alternate Hypothesis (H1): There is significant relationship between income level and brand preference of laptop.

4. **Null Hypothesis (H0):** There is no significant relationship between price and brand preference of laptop.

   Alternate Hypothesis (H1): There is significant relationship between price and brand preference of laptop.

5. **Null Hypothesis (H0):** There is no significant relationship between Performance and brand preference of laptop.

   Alternate Hypothesis (H1): There is significant relationship between Performance and brand preference of laptop.

6. **Null Hypothesis (H0):** There is no significant relationship between brand value and brand preference of laptop.

   Alternate Hypothesis (H1): There is significant relationship between brand value and brand preference of laptop.

7. **Null Hypothesis (H0):** There is no significant relationship between features available in the laptop and brand preference of laptop.

   Alternate Hypothesis (H1): There is significant relationship between features available in the laptop and brand preference of laptop.

8. **Null Hypothesis (H0):** There is no significant relationship between after sales services and brand preference of laptop.

Alternate Hypothesis (H1): There is significant relationship between after sales services and brand preference of laptop.

Chapter 2: Literature Review

Various brands of laptops are available from which the consumers can choose any brand as their requirement and need. But which brand the consumers either it is the student, professional prefers the most, is what this survey tries to find out. There has been various research conducted regarding the brand preference of laptop, which focuses to know about the awareness of brands of laptop available among the consumers and their preference of laptops.

A research "Brand Preference of Laptops among MBA students" was conducted by Gauri Aryal of Ace Institute of Management, Sinamangal for the award of MBA degree. She has conducted this research to find out the brand awareness of laptop among MBA students. For which she have selected the samples of 100 students and have collected the information through questionnaire. The major objectives of her research were to study the brand preference of laptops among the MBA students, to study how much the brand of laptop is penetrated in the mind of students and to determine the perception of students regarding the brand of laptop.

The major findings of this research are most preferable brand of laptop among the user is Dell, Acer, most of the respondents would like to own Dell laptop in future and the parameters influencing the purchase of the laptops as per are Performance, features, Price, offers and promotion.

Another research was conducted by Prashant Kumar as "Brand preference of laptops in students" for the award of MBA degree. And the major findings of his research are most of the respondents are brand loyal to their preferred brand despite of price and HP and Compaq are most preferred brand of laptops.

Chapter 3: Research Methodology

3.1 TYPES OF RESEARCH/ DESIGN

This research is both quantitative and exploratory in nature as it will try to explore different issues related to brand preference of laptop and several factors influencing the choice of particular brand of laptop. It is an applied research as it aims of using the existing theory rather than developing the new one and helps to improve understanding of the subject. Questionnaire is prepared and the link is filled online by the respondents to collect the information in this survey.

3.2 DATA SOURCES

Both primary and secondary sources of data are used to conduct the research.

3.2.1 PRIMARY DATA

Primary data were collected by Questionnaire prepared online and the link is filled online by the respondents to collect the information. Self- administered questionnaire were used. Information was collected online so the information is confidential.

3.2.2 SECONDARY DATA

Secondary information was obtained from various sources:

- Websites
- Newspapers
- Books
- Articles
- Previous reports on similar topic

3.3 QUESTIONNAIRES

Both structured and unstructured questionnaires are used for the survey. Regarding administering the questionnaires both self-administered and interviewer administered methods were used. In self-administered method, emails were used and questionnaires were distributed and collected and as for interviewer administered, telephone survey questionnaire was used. Questionnaire consisted of various types of questions such as ranking scale, rating scale, single response questions, multiple response questions, LIKERT scale and others.

3.4 SCALES

This survey aims to identify the brand preference of laptop so attitude scale has been used as it helps to identify people's perception, behaviors towards other things. Under the attitude scale various other scales are used like:

3.4.1 SIMPLE ATTITUDE SCALE

- Dichotomous scale
- Multiple choice, single response scale
- Multiple choice, multiple response scale

3.4.2 LIKERT SCALE

Likert scale was also used for the purpose of the study. Here the respondents were required to indicate a degree of agreement and disagreement with each series of statement. Each scale item had five response categories ranging from strongly agree to strongly disagree. Five point scales was used.

3.5 SAMPLING DESIGN

In this research the non-probability sampling technique was used. Under this technique convenience sampling was used. The respondent was selected as per my convenience and without any restrictions covering different institution and groups.

The total number of sample size used is 100 to conduct the research. The sample was then divided into the groups on the basis of gender, education background, income, occupation etc.

3.6 DATA COLLECTION METHODS

The data collection is self-administered where the Questionnaire was prepared online and the link is filled online by the respondents to collect the information. Information was collected online so the information is confidential.

3.7 DATA MANAGEMENT AND ANALYSIS

In this research, for the calculation of data software like: SPSS, MS word, MS excels are used. Similarly, for the data analysis descriptive analysis and inferential analysis is used. For descriptive analysis frequency and percentage table, mean, standard deviation etc are used and for inferential analysis chi-square test, t-test, ANOVA test etc are used.

Chapter 4: Data Analysis

This research is an exploratory type; the researcher has tried to provide perception and preferences of the students of any sector. Considering minimum 100 respondents was the target but some of the data may be invalid due to errors. So, there are 115 respondents who are considered as the final consumer.

4.1 DESCRIPTIVE STATISTICS (FREQUENCIES ANALYSIS)

Descriptive statistics aims to summarize a data and describe the basic features of the data in a study all together to summaries about the sample and the measures. Below shows the details of the respondents according to various socio- demographic variables:

4.1.1 GENDER OF RESPONDENTS

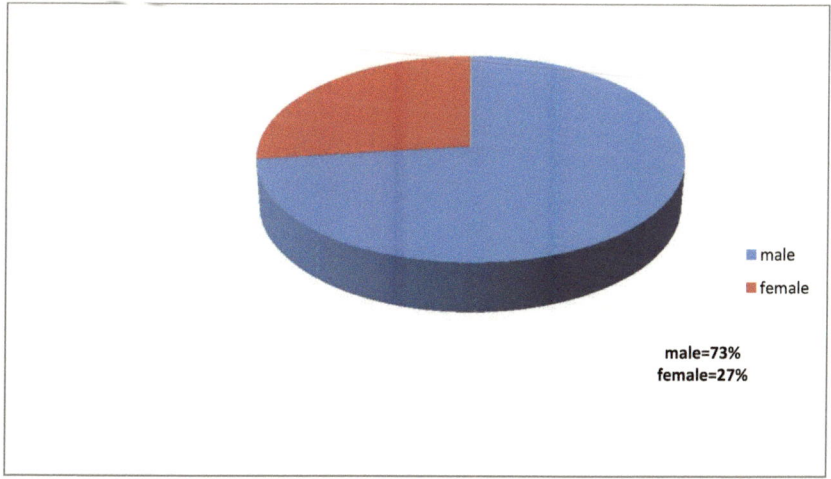

male=73%
female=27%

Figure 2: Pie chart representing Gender

The above figure 2 shows the total number of respondents who participated in this survey as per the gender. Out of total 100 samples, there are 73 males and 27 females, which make 73 % male and 27% female.

4.1.2 EDUCATIONAL BACKGROUND OF RESPONDENTS

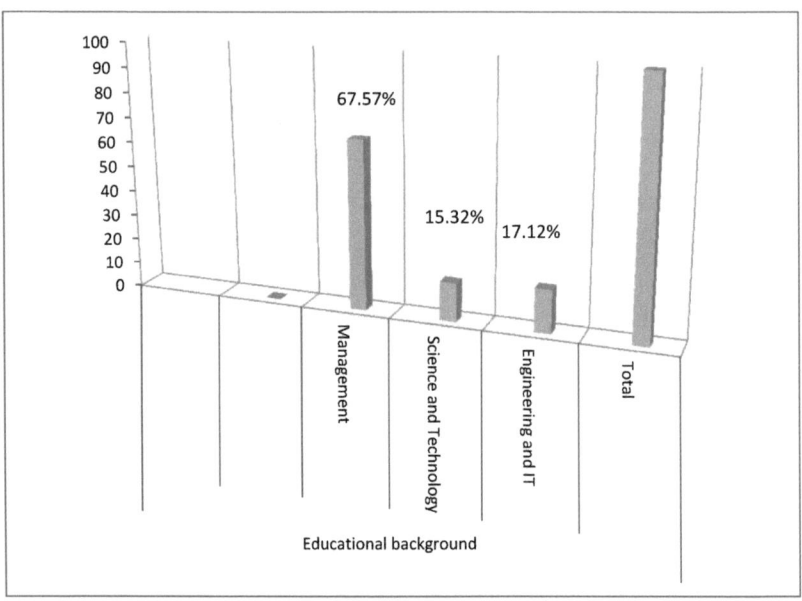

Figure 3: Bar chart representing Educational Background

The above figure 3 shows the total number of respondents who participated in this survey as per the Educational Background. Out of total 100 respondents, 69% were of Management background, 13% were of Science and technology and 18% were of Engineering & technology background.

4.1.3 FAMILY OCCUPATION

Family main Occupation	Frequency	Percent
Agriculture	9	7.8
Business person	47	40.9
Self employed personnel	17	14.8
Service	35	30.4
Others	7	6.1
Total	115	100

Table 1: Frequency distribution of Family Main Occupation

According to the table 1, the total number of students having Laptops has Businessperson as a Family's main Occupation which is 40.9%. ,followed by Service which is 30.4%, Self-employed professional which is 14.8%, Agriculture which is 7.8% and others 6.1% respectively.

4.1.4 POST OF RESPONDENTS

Post	Frequency	Percent
Junior level	25	22.7
middle level	57	51.8
senior level	16	14.5
Businessperson	12	10.9
Total	110	100

Table 2: Frequency distribution of Income level

According to the table 2, the total number of students having Laptops employed at middle level is highest which is 51.8%. ,followed by Junior level which is 22.7%,senior level 14.5% and business person which is 10.9%,5 respondents do not have job nor business,so it is not included in determining the post of respondents..

4.1.5 INCOME LEVEL OF RESPONDENTS

Income	Frequency	Percent
less than 10000	22	23
10000-20000	46	47
20000-30000	12	12
30000 and above	17	18
Total	97	100

Table 3: Frequency distribution of Income level

According to the table 3, highest frequency of income level is within 10000 – 20000 which is 47%. Since, the respondents are students, 23% of them are not working or have income level less than 10000, 18% earned above 30000 and 12% earn within 20000-30000 respectively.

4.1.6 PREFERRED BRAND OF LAPTOPS

Brand	Frequency	Percent
Dell	56	49
HP	13	11
samsung	3	3
sony	1	1
lenovo	11	10
Apple	14	12
acer	10	9
Total	108	94
Others	7	6
Total	115	100

Table 4: Frequency distribution of Brand preference of Laptops.

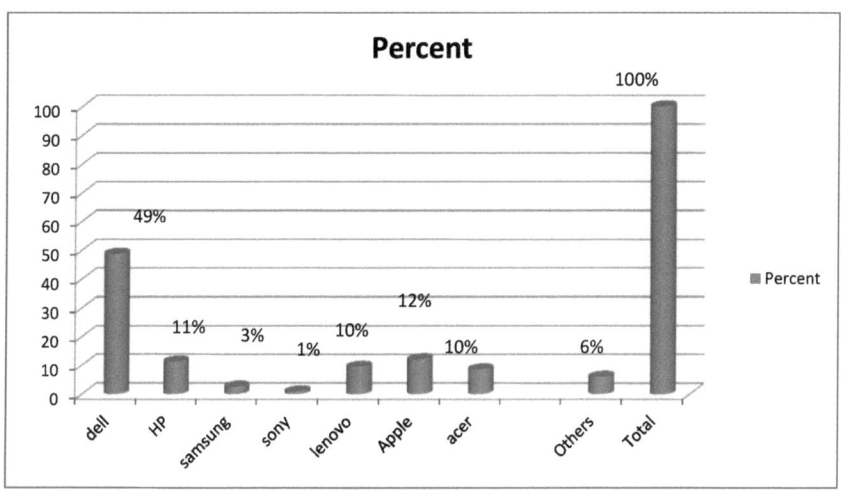

Figure 4: Percentage distribution of Brand preference of Laptops

In table 4 and figure 4, it can be made clear that maximum number of Laptops used by students is of Dell which is 49%. Second highest used laptop is of Apple which is 12%, followed by HP 11% , Acer and Lenovo with 10%,3% Samsung with 4% ,Sony 1% and others 6% respectively.

4.1.7 COST OF LAPTOPS

Cost of your Laptop		
Cost	Frequency	Percent
less than 40000	10	9
40000-60000	62	55
60000-80000	22	19
above 80000	19	17
Total	113	100

Table 5: Frequency distribution of Cost of Laptops.

According to the table 5, the highest frequency of costs of laptops preferred by students are between 40000-60000 which is 55%, followed by range between 60000-80000 which is 19%, above 80000 which is 17% and less than 40000 which is 9% respectively.

4.2 Inferential Statistics (Chi-square test)

Inferential statistics is used to make inferences from the data to more general conditions and reach conclusions that extent beyond the immediate data alone.

4.2.1 GENDER AND BRAND PREFERENCE OF LAPTOPS

Cross tabulation between Gender and Brand Preference of Laptops

Laptop	Brands		dell	HP	samsung	sony	lenovo	Apple	acer	Total
Gender	Male	Count	41	10	2	1	8	13	6	81
		%	50.60%	12.30%	2.50%	1.20%	9.90%	16.00%	7.40%	100.00%
	Female	Count	15	3	1	0	3	1	4	27
		%	55.60%	11.10%	3.70%	0.00%	11.10%	3.70%	14.80%	100.00%
Total		Count	56	13	3	1	11	14	10	108
		%	51.90%	12.00%	2.80%	0.90%	10.20%	13.00%	9.30%	100.00%

Table 5: Cross tabulation between Gender and Brand Preference of Laptops

Out of 81 male respondents, 50.6% preferred Dell, 12.3% preferred HP, 2.5% Preferred Samsung, 1.2% preferred Sony, 9.9% preferred Lenovo, 16% preferred Apple and 7.4% prefer Acer. Similarly, out of 15 female respondents, 55.6% used Dell, 11.1% used HP, 3.7% used Samsung, 11.1% used Lenovo, 3.7% used Apple and 14.8% used Acer.

Chi-Square Tests			
	Value	df	Asymp. Sig. (2-sided)
Pearson Chi-Square	4.177a	6	0.653

Table 6: Chi-square test of Gender and Brand Preference of Laptops

18

Here, P-value is 0.653 which is greater than our significance level i.e. 0.05. Therefore, we do not reject H0.There is no significant relationship between gender and brand preference of Laptops among the students.

4.2.2 FAMILY OCCUPATION AND BRAND PREFERENCE OF LAPTOPS

Family Main Occupation * Which Laptop Pc you use/prefer? Crosstabulation										
Laptop			dell	HP	samsung	sony	lenovo	Apple	acer	Total
	Agriculture	Count	4	0	0	0	2	0	0	6
Family		%	67%	0%	0%	0%	33%	0%	0%	100%
Main	Business person	Count	31	3	0	0	1	7	3	45
Occupation		%	69%	7%	0%	0%	2%	16%	7%	100%
	Self employed	Count	2	1	1	0	5	6	2	17
		%	12%	6%	6%	0%	29%	35%	12%	100%
	Service	Count	15	8	1	1	3	1	4	33
		%	46%	24%	3%	3%	9%	3%	12%	100%
Total		Count	52	12	2	1	11	14	9	101
		%	52%	12%	2%	1%	11%	14%	9%	100%

Table 7: Cross tabulation between Family Occupation & Brand Preference of Laptops

Out of 6 respondents with agriculture as family's main occupation 67% preferred Dell and 33% Lenovo. Out of 31 respondents with Businessperson family's occupation highest used laptop is Dell with 69%,7%/HP,2% Lenovo,16% Apple and 7% acer. Out of 33 respondents Service family's occupation highest used is Dell with 46%,24% HP,Samsung and sony being 3% ,Lenovo 9%, Apple 3% and acer 12%. Out of 17 respondents with Self-employed professional family's occupation highest preferred laptops are Apple with 35% and Lenovo with 29% respectively.

Chi-Square Tests			
	Value	df	Asymp. Sig. (2-sided)
Pearson Chi-Square	41.431a	18	0.001

Table 8: Chi-square test of Family Occupation & Brand Preference of Laptops

Here, P-value is 0.001 which is less than significance level i.e. 0.05. Therefore, we reject H0. There is significant relationship between Family Main Occupation and Brand Preference of Laptops.

4.2.3 INCOME LEVEL AND BRAND PREFERENCE OF LAPTOPS

Crosstabulation of income and laptop									
Income	Laptop	dell	HP	samsung	sony	lenovo	Apple	acer	Total
less than 10000	Count	16	1	0	0	1	0	1	19
	%	84%	5%	0%	0%	5%	0%	5%	100%
10000-20000	Count	29	6	0	0	6	0	5	46
	%	63%	13%	0%	0%	13%	0%	11%	100%
20000-30000	Count	1	3	3	0	2	2	1	12
	%	8%	25%	25%	0%	17%	17%	8%	100%
30000 and above	Count	2	0	0	1	1	12	0	16
	%	13%	0%	0%	6%	6%	75%	0%	100%

Table 9: Cross tabulation between Income level and Brand Preference of Laptops

The above table shows the Cross tabulation between income level and brand preference of laptops among the students. Students having the income level of 10000-20000 are 46 have the highest numbers of laptops within which 63% preferred Dell, 14.30% used HP, 2.9% used Samsung, 8.60% used Sony, 20% used Lenovo, 2.90% used Apple and 20% used Acer. Out of 28 respondents with less than 10000 income 32.10% preferred Dell, 14.30% used HP, 7.10%

used Samsung, 10.70% used Sony, 10.70% used Lenovo, 10.70% used Apple and 14.30% used Acer. Similarly, The respondents having income of 20000-30000 and above 30000 are 13 each. In range of 20000-30000 Dell and Apple is most preferred with 23.10% and in range of above 30000 Dell, HP and Apple is most preferred with 23.10%.

4.2.4 PRICE LEVEL AND BRAND PREFERENCE OF LAPTOPS

Crosstabulation of Cost and preference of Laptop

Laptop			Dell	HP	samsung	sony	lenovo	Apple	acer	Total
Cost	less than 40000	Count	6	1	0	0	1	0	2	10
		%	60%	10%	0%	0%	10%	0%	20%	100%
	40000-60000	Count	41	7	1	0	5	0	4	58
		%	71%	12%	2%	0%	9%	0%	7%	100%
	60000-80000	Count	6	4	1	1	5	1	3	21
		%	29%	19%	5%	5%	24%	5%	14%	100%
	above 80000	Count	1	1	1	0	0	13	1	17
		%	6%	6%	6%	0%	0%	77%	6%	100%
Total		Count	54	13	3	1	11	14	10	106
		%	51%	12%	3%	1%	10%	13%	9%	100%

Table 10: Cross tabulation between Price level and Brand Preference of Laptops

The above table shows the relationship between Price (Cost) of laptops and brand preference of laptops. Out of 10 respondents who spent less than 40000 to buy laptop, 60% of them preferred Dell, acer by 20%, HP and Lenovo is preferred by 10% each. Out of 48 respondents who spent 40000-60000 to buy laptop, 71% buy Dell, 12% bought HP,7% bought Acer and 2% Samsung.. Out of 21 respondents who spent 60000-80000 to buy laptop, 29% bought Dell, 19% bought HP, 5% bought Sony and samsung, 24% bought Lenovo, 5% bought Apple and 14% bought Acer. Out of 17 respondents who spent above 80000 to buy laptop, 6% bought Dell, HP,acer and Samsung each and 77% bought Apple.

Chi-Square Tests			
	Value	df	Asymp. Sig. (2-sided)
Pearson Chi-Square	89.802a	18	0

Table 11: Chi-square test of Price level and Brand Preference of Laptops

Here, P-value is 0 which is less than significance level i.e. 0.05. So, we reject H0. Therefore, there is significant relationship between Price level and Brand Preference of Laptops.

4.3 ANOVA (F-TEST)

4.3.1 LIKERT SCALE

	N	Mean	Std. Deviation
dell	56	3.98	0.52
HP	13	3.85	1.28
samsung	3	4	0.00
lenovo	11	2.91	1.58
Apple	14	4.36	1.08
acer	10	3.5	0.71
Total	108	3.87	0.95

Table 12: Average of satisfaction of features

Apple has the highest mean value for satisfaction of features which means the respondents are highly satisfied with the features of Apple, followed by samsung Dell, HP, Lenovo, Acer and respectively.Lenovo has highest variation.

Satisfied with Features						
	Sum of Squares	df	Mean Square	F	Sig.	
Between Groups	16.887	6	2.815	3.585	0.003	
Within Groups	79.298	101	0.785			
Total	96.185	107				

Table 13: One-way ANOVA between satisfaction with Features and Brand preference of laptops

Here, P-value is 0.003 which is < 0.05, so we reject null hypothesis. Therefore, there is significant relationship between features and brand preference of laptops among the students.

Satisfied with After Sales Services

	N	Mean	Std. Deviation
dell	50	3.55	0.737
HP	13	3.46	1.33
samsung	3	3.67	1.155
sony	1	5	.
lenovo	11	2.64	1.362
Apple	14	4.21	1.251
acer	10	3.4	0.966
Total	108	3.54	1.054

Table 14: Average of satisfaction of After Sales Service

Here, the mean of Apple is higher than other mean value which shows the respondents are highly satisfied with the after sales services of Apple. The mean value of Dell,Samsung,acer and HP is followed by Lenovo.

Satisfied with After Sales Services					
	Sum of Squares	df	Mean Square	F	Sig.
Between Groups	17.813	6	2.969	2.968	0.01
Within Groups	101.039	101	1		
Total	118.852	107			

Table 15: One-way ANOVA between satisfaction with after sales services and Brand preference of laptops

Hereby, P-value is 0.01 which is < 0.05, so we reject null hypothesis. Therefore, there is significant relationship between after sales services and brand preference of laptops among the students.

satisfaction of Brand	N	Mean	Std. Deviation
dell	56	3.88	0.507
HP	13	4	0.707
samsung	3	4	1
sony	1	5	.
lenovo	11	3.36	1.362
Apple	14	4.29	1.139
acer	9	4	0.5
Total	107	3.92	0.791

Table 16: Average of satisfaction of Brand value

The mean value of Apple has the highest value so; the respondents are highly satisfied with the brand value of Apple followed by HP,Samsung and acer.

	Sum of Squares	df	Mean Square	F	Sig.
Between Groups	6.715	6	1.119	1.88	0.092
Within Groups	59.528	100	0.595		
Total	66.243	106			

Table 17: One-way ANOVA between satisfaction with Brand value and Brand preference of laptops

Here, P-value is 0.092 which is < 0.05, so we reject null hypothesis. Therefore, there is significant relationship between brand value and brand preference of laptops among the students.

Satisfied with Outlook	N	Mean	Std. Deviation
dell	56	3.88	0.634
HP	13	3.69	0.751
samsung	3	3.67	1.155
lenovo	11	3.55	1.368
Apple	14	4.5	1.16
acer	10	4	0.667
Total	108	3.91	0.86

Table 18: Average of satisfaction of Outlook

The most preferred outlook is of Apple because it has the highest mean and the least preferred outlook is of Lenovo. Dell has the least deviation for outlook and Lenovo has the highest deviation.

ANOVA					
Satisfied with Outlook					
	Sum of Squares	df	Mean Square	F	Sig.
Between Groups	7.286	6	1.214	1.708	0.127
Within Groups	71.788	101	0.711		
Total	79.074	107			

Table 19: One-way ANOVA between satisfaction with outlook and Brand preference of laptops

Here, P-value is 0.134 which is > 0.05, so we do not reject null hypothesis. Therefore, there is no significant relationship between outlook and brand preference of laptops among the students.

Satisfied with its Performance			
	N	Mean	Std. Deviation
dell	56	3.95	0.616
HP	13	4.31	0.751
samsung	3	3.33	0.577
sony	1	5	.
lenovo	11	4.09	1.64
Apple	14	4.5	1.16
acer	10	3.5	0.972
Total	108	4.03	0.922

Table 20: Average of satisfaction of Performance

The respondents are highly satisfied with the performance of Apple, it has the highest mean i.e. 4.5. The least preferred brand for performance is Samsung. Samsung has the low deviation whereas Lenovo has the high deviation on performance.

ANOVA					
Satisfied with its Performance					
	Sum of Squares	df	Mean Square	F	Sig.
Between Groups	9.732	6	1.622	2.018	0.07
Within Groups	81.184	101	0.804		
Total	90.917	107			

Table 21: One-way ANOVA between satisfaction with performance and Brand preference of laptops

Here, P-value is 0.07 which is not equal to 0.05, so we reject null hypothesis. Therefore, there is significant relationship between performance and brand preference of laptops among the students.

Average of satisfaction variables	Mean
Satisfied with Features	3.83
Satisfied with After Sales Services	3.45
Satisfied with The Brand	3.92
Satisfied with Outlook	3.91
Satisfied with its Performance	4.03

Table 22: Average of satisfaction variables

Out of 100 respondents, they are highly satisfied with the performance of the laptop and the least satisfied variable is after sales services.

Brand preference of Laptop	Mean
Rank of Dell	3.14
Rank of Apple	4.01
Rank of Lenovo	3.64
Rank of Acer	3.52
Rank of HP	3.5

Table 23: Ranking the brand preference of Laptops

According to the above table the most preferred brand of laptop is of Apple, second preferred brand is Lenovo, third ranked is Acer, fourth ranked is HP, fifth is apple and sixth ranked is Dell.

Chapter 5: Conclusion

Among the 100 respondents 73% of male and 27% of female respondents were taken. Among them maximum were those whose family's main occupation is businessperson, then service, then self-employed professional, then agriculture and students. Most of them were from the management educational backgrounds i.e. 67.57%, 17.12% were from engineering and IT background and remaining i.e. 15.32% were from science and technology . Majority of the respondent's income is within the range of 10000-20000 with 47%, while the income 20000-30000 with only 12%. Most of the respondent's cost of their laptop lies within 40000-60000 62% and there were only10% whose cost of laptop is less than 40000. The most used brand of laptop is of Dell followed by Apple, then by HP and acer then Lenovo, Samsung and sony respectively.

Majority of respondents who have service as their family's main occupation preferred Dell and Self-employed has the least respondents. Majority of respondents were from the income group of Rs 10000-20000. Among them most preferred Dell with 63%, then HP and Lenovo, then Acer. At price range of 40000-60000, majority of respondents are willing to buy the laptop Dell at 71%. But at price above 80000, Apple is most preferred.

Most of the respondents who are the user of Apple laptops are highly satisfied with the features, after sales services, brand value, outlook and performance. But the respondents of Samsung are not satisfied with Performance and Lenovo features, after sales services, brand value, outlook.

According to the research, there is no significant relationship between gender and brand preference of laptops. There is significant relationship between Family main occupation and brand preference of laptops. There is significant relationship between Income level and brand preference of laptops. There is significant relationship between price level and brand preference of laptops. There is significant relationship between features and brand preference of laptops. There is significant relationship between after sales services and brand preference of laptops. There is significant relationship between brand value and brand preference of laptops. There is significant relationship between outlook and brand preference of laptops. There is significant relationship between performance and brand preference of laptops.

Bibliography

1. Pant, Prem R., & Wolff, Howard.K (2005 A.D). A Hand book for Social science Research and Thesis Writing. Kathmandu. Buddha Academic Publishers & Distributor Pvt. Ltd
2. Zikmund William (2007 A.D). Business Research Method 7th Edition. Australia. Thomas Press